The Haunting
of the Snarkasbord

Feeling the heat in a cannibal's cauldron are, from right to left, August A. Imholtz, Jr., Alison Tannebaum, and Byron W. Sewell.

The Haunting of the Snarkasbord

A Portmanteau inspired by Lewis Carroll's
The Hunting of the Snark

by Alison Tannenbaum
Byron W. Sewell
Charlie Lovett and
August A. Imholtz, Jr

ILLUSTRATIONS BY
BYRON W. SEWELL

evertype
2012

Published by Evertype, Cnoc Sceichín, Leac an Anfa, Cathair na Mart, Co. Mhaigh Eo, Éire. *www.evertype.com*.

ISBN-10 1-904808-98-0
ISBN-13 978-1-904808-98-5

Typeset in De Vinne Text, Mona Lisa, ENGRAVERS' ROMAN, and *Liberty* by Michael Everson.

Illustrations: Byron W. Sewell.

Cover: Michael Everson and Byron W. Sewell.

Printed by LightningSource.

Foreword

$\mathcal{S}$ometimes a publisher is given a gift for his unbirthday. Not long ago, four noted Carrollians came to me with a proposal for a dark, humorous parody of *The Hunting of the Snark* concerning what followed the Baker's vanishing and the Crew's continued hunt for a snark on Snark Island. How could one refuse?

Alison Tannenbaum wrote the poetry in *Snarkasbord: A Crewsome Choice* and also wrote notes on Byron W. Sewell's illustrations for it. An introduction and Gardnerian-style notes have been written by August A. Imholtz, Jr in his inimitable style.

This edition marks the first public publication of the poems "The Booking", "The Recrewting", and "The Sailing"—the three "Missing Fits" composed by Charlie Lovett. These were originally written for a secret English Snarkian Society, and were mentioned by Selwyn Goodacre in his "The Listing of the *Snark*" in Martin Gardner's final version of *The Annotated Hunting of the Snark*. Hitherto, they have only ever been seen by the members or guests of the Society.

In addition to his wonderful illustrations, Byron W. Sewell has contributed an original short story, "Forks and Soap", which tells what happened to the Baker from the viewpoint of the Boojum. Like Lovett's parodies, this short story has never before been seen by the public; it was issued in a very limited number to his Carrollian friends.

If you have been lucky enough to get hold of *The Haunting of the Snarkasbord* but have never read *The Hunting of the Snark*, please see page 148.

Michael Everson
Westport, April 2012

Contents

Snarkasbord:
A Crewsome Choice

AN AGONY IN NINE FITS

BY

ALISON TANNENBAUM

INTRODUCTION BY
AUGUST A. IMHOLTZ, JR

ILLUSTRATIONS BY
BYRON W. SEWELL

Introduction

According to C. L. Dodgson's diary entry for 21 January 1868,[1] he had attended on the previous evening, as a guest of one of the members, perhaps Peter Lund Simmonds,[2] his one and only meeting at the notorious Cannibal Club in London. He recorded without elaboration the utter revulsion brought on by that dinner party: "The hour I spent dining yesterday at that heinous society led by the reprobate Burton will haunt me forever. It was, truly, a Black Stone day."[3] No other reference to the infamous Cannibal Club appears in Dodgson's surviving diaries or letters and this is not surprising, given the group's irreverent

---

1   Edward Wakeling, editor. *Lewis Carroll's Diaries.* Vol. 5, September 1864 to January 1868. (Luton: The Lewis Carroll Society, 1999) p. 381-b.

2   Peter Lund Simmonds (1814-1897), a Dane by birth, was a journalist who married Ellen Mary Molesworth. He had been a seaman, a self-taught engineer, and publisher of *The Technologist: a Monthly Record of Science Applied to Art and Manufacture* and it was in that regard that he came to know Dodgson. He also wrote the unjustly neglected *The Curiosities of Food; or the Dainties or Delicacies of Different Nations Obtained from the Animal Kingdom.*

3   The phrase "Black Stone Day" refers not to the Roman practice of marking a calendar day with a piece of white chalk but rather to the

nature and factious membership—many were Cambridge men.

The Cannibal Club was founded in 1863 as a dining club for the more anti-establishment and totally unconventional members of the Royal Anthropological Society. Dr. James Hunt, the president of the Anthropological Society, was its first chairman and among its early members were the famous linguist, explorer, and sexual adventurer Sir Richard Burton as well as the self-flagellating poet Charles Algernon Swinburne. In his monograph *Books on the Table* Edmund Gosse described a meeting of the club in this way:

> The Cannibal Club met at Bartolini's Hotel, near Leicester Square, close to the Society's meeting-room in St. Martin's Place. It dined in front of a mace, which represented the ebony head of a negro gnawing the ivory thigh-bone of a man. To this object Swinburne irreverently gave the name "Ecce Homo"; it was always placed on the dinner-table opposite the president.[4]

In addition to much discussion of cannibalism over dinner, if not its outright practice—even Bartolini's chef had his limits, and other anthropological curiosities, considerable attention was devoted as well to pornography from rituals of India to polygamous practices in Utah's Salt Lake City. All or any of those would have been enough to horrify Charles Lutwidge Dodgson; but it was surely the recitation of Swinburne's "Cannibal Catechism,"[5]—a virulent attack on

---

practice of the ancient Greeks of putting a white stone in one jar or a black stone in another jar at the end of a day to record the number of days that had been either good or bad, respectively.

4   Edmund Gosse, *Books on the Table*. (New York: Scribners, 1921) p. 64.

5   The catechism is too offensive to reprint here. It was privately printed in London in 1913.

the sanctity of the Eucharist—that caused him to fly out of Bartolini's Hotel's front door as fast as he could.

The memory of that horrific evening may well have terrorized Dodgson's waking and sleeping hours for decades and could well have brought him to compose, as a kind of exorcism of the Cannibal Club from his mind and heart, the manuscript published here for the first time. Since the narrative appears to be a macabre sequel to his masterful nonsense epyllion, *The Hunting of the Snark*, we must posit for its composition a date sometime after 1876 and of course before his death in early1898.

The text of *Snarkasbord* as we have in a manuscript written in purple ink in a tan paper-covered school exercise book was found by the distinguished Lewis Carroll collector Victoria Grossman in Birmingham last March. She had come to Birmingham with her husband Byron, who was serving as a consultant with British Polyurethane Ltd in their efforts to develop a new line of absorbent but transparent meat-packaging membranes. While she was wandering from antiquarian book shop to book shop, she came upon an auction in progress at the stately old house of Fiddle and Webb Ltd, Auctioneers and Valuers. What Lewis Carroll books there were to be had went for vast sums to rival Carroll collectors, mostly to an intense bidder from Swadlincote who sported a baker's hat and a sharp collector from London, who may not have been as young as he appeared.

Victoria decided to bid on a cache of nineteenth-century school exercise books, which she thought would be thoroughly devoid of interest, but she loved the speckled accordion cardboard box in which they had been stuffed more than half a century ago and got the lot for £7.20. On closer examination, she observed that the handwriting in one of the battered and faded exercise books looked intriguingly like the idiosyncratic cursive printing Lewis Carroll had used in the original draft of his book that became the children's classic story *Alice's Adventures in Wonderland*. Like Morris L. Parrish, her predecessor in Carroll collecting, she decided to print a limited edition of the work she had discovered much as Parrish had for Dodgson's 1867 diary of a *Trip to Russia*. She contacted a small caucus of members of the Lewis Carroll Society of North America and after months of intense though never strident negotiations, a publishing task force consisting of B. Ryan Swell, III, A. Lissom-Tanner, and Arthur Ausholz was formed. The manuscript was edited and prepared for publication, discursive explanatory notes were added, and illustrations, where none had existed before, were created especially for this Evertype edition, the first edition of *Snarkasbord*, a masterpiece which may or may not be the work of Charles Lutwidge Dodgson, otherwise known as Lewis Carroll.

August A. Imholtz. Jr
Beltsville, April 2012

Fit I
The Threat of Famine

The Threat of Famine

"We have sailed many months, we have sailed many
  weeks,
    Four weeks to the month you may mark.
But never as yet ('tis your captain who speaks)
    Have we caught the least glimpse of a Snark."

But all of this changed on a dark, gloomy night,
    The night they saw Baker expire.
He'd vanished away, was gone, out of sight.
    His Boojum, he ate him, entire!

No one need tell you just how it occurred;

    The sight was too much to behold.

He'd been eaten alive, we (ghastly!) observed,

    And the trail to more Snarks had run cold.

Despite this disaster, the crew was still brave,

    Determined to live by their code:

To bring home a Snark, which (with soap) they would
lave,

    Ere it bloat up, decay, and explode.

Although the old map that they'd brought had no
marks,

    They'd reckoned the latitude right:

At forty-two north, they'd thought to find Snarks,

    At longitude nearest to night.

The party was left with a shortage of stores;

    Not did one mouldy bagel remain.

A plan must be made to survive on these shores,

    Lest they all go quite fully insane.

In some despair, the crew turned to their Bellman,

    Lest each one become a revenant.

A word that they'd heard (in use) only seldom,

    And really knew not what it meant.

An assessment was made of the plight they were in;

    The Bellman took charge of the task.

The meat they had left was in one tiny tin,

    Too meager for nine, lest you ask.

The only solution the Bellman could see

    Was to start eating crewmen: Oh, my!

But how to dispatch one? (A killer to be?)

    And how would one choose who's to die?

But Fate may assist us, and help us to find

    The Snark that we've sought all this time.

We'll encounter strange things of a dangerous kind,

    That could kill each of us in our prime!

Fit II
The Billiard-Marker
and the Boar Pit

The Billiard-Marker
and the Boar Pit

With luck unexpected, a tragedy dark
    Felled the Billiard-Marker quite soon.
A trap for wild boars, dug by hunters (not Snark!)
    Scored the poor fellow: A boon!

The Butcher took charge of the corpse and he sliced
    The flesh into quarters and flanks.
Bellman seasoned the meat, and potatoes he riced;
    The fire well-roasted the shanks.

The holes from the spikes tenderized the tough meat.

　　Fish sauce helped cover the smell,

And pineapple juice made it all nice and sweet.

　　The Snark hunters liked it quite well.

The Bellman was proud of his efforts to date,

　　And his cooking skills just grew and grew.

Of the meals that they ate, all were first rate.

　　He said: "What we eat thrice is stew!"

[The Beaver, of course, did not care to partake.

　　He subsisted on turnips and kale.

He'd never tried meat; it would be a mistake.

　　'Twould curl up a flat beaver-tail!]

The stew well-sustained them while searching for
Snark,
For energy while on the march.
They searched all around in the forest and park;
Near every black pine and tall larch.

The weeks wore on, dismal, no Snarks were in sight.
Some Jubjubs, with fine Pinot Noir,
But no sign of a Snark, by day or at night.
They longed for some steak, served tartare!

Fit III
The Banker and the Cliff

The Banker
and the Cliff

While traipsing along in pursuit of a Snark,
　　The Banker had tripped on his coat.
He fell off a sheer cliff in the gloom and the dark.
　　He was dead as a second-hand note!

They wrapped up the Banker, and dragged him to
　　camp.
　　Through forest and quicksand-filled bogs,
They struggled along, though their clothes were all
　　damp.
　　The Butcher had packed him with frogs.

The recipe this time was different, by far:

Mango and spices exotic.

Fresh Banker-kabobs, broiled with lizards and gar.

The aroma was quite hypnotic.

For forty-two meals, the Baker's meat lasted.

All Snarks were still way too reclusive.

They found lemurs, apes, and pythons (who fasted).

No sign of a Snark, how elusive!

Fit IV
The Bonnet-Maker
in the Mangroves

The Bonnet-Maker in the Mangroves

The Bonnet-maker's fate was next to befall.
    He slipped and fell into the brine.
He sank 'mongst the mangroves, no swimming at all.
    The crew dragged his corpse out with a pine.

They trundled him back to their camp in the woods.
    The Butcher carved sirloins and hams.
He soaked them in brandy (a part of their goods),
    And added hot peppers and yams.

Two days on the fire, the feast was all cooked.

The crewmen did salivate and moan.

After only one taste, on this they were hooked!

It was better than bœuf bourguignon.

The leftover meat tasted just like fresh pork,

So they sliced up a ham, a good bunch.

With mustard and cress, piled on with a fork,

The sandwiches made a nice lunch!

Back to the dark jungle, they struggled again

In search of some Snarks (even one!).

They moved along faster than when they were ten,

But, still, they were not nearly done.

Fit V
The Barrister Finds Honey

F I T   T H E   F I F T H

The Barrister Finds Honey

As they hurried along through vines and tall trees,
　　The Barrister smelled something sweet.
He tried to take honey from some nasty bees,
　　And got quite badly stung, on his feet.

He fell to the ground, both in shock and in pain,
　　His countenance sickly and pale.
The crew tried first-aid, at once, and again;
　　Their efforts were to no avail.

The crew, with great care, took the honey away,

Scaring the bees with swamp gas.

They viewed the big Barrister's corpse with dismay.

What were they to do with this mass?

Now cut down to five, the small crew was aghast.

This dead, blimp-like corpse was huge!

They struggled and strained to get back to camp fast.

The Butcher took charge of the stooge.

The meal was prepared, the components all stewed

With ginger and pampas-grass root.

For forty-two hours, it simmered and brewed,

To sustain them in endless pursuit.

[The Bellman was sure he'd come up with a win

To store meat from the Barrister's hulk.

He'd make some pâté, and, to seal every tin,

Use Barrister-blubber, in bulk.]

Into the dark jungle, the crew went again,

Their resolve and energy stronger.

With thimbles and hope, along marched the men,

Hoping: "Snark!" before too much longer.

Fit VI
The Broker Encounters
the Toad

The Broker Encounters the Toad

The Broker soon spied a large, bulgy toad,
    Its eyes of dark black were so bright!
One little touch his life's end soon forbode:
    Bufagins too potent to fight.

He soon felt quite ill, and fell far behind.
    He was weak and could no longer walk.
The group finally missed him, and came back to find
    The Broker, unable to talk!

They poked and they prodded him, to no avail.

They tickled him under his nose.

But try as they might, they were destined to fail:

He was dead and quite stuck in one pose.

The crew could not waste this windfall of fresh meat,

But feared that the poison in place

Would need to be purged before they could eat.

The Butcher, he worked all apace.

He braised it with honey; he boiled it in beer.

He added soft soap and guar.

He watched it and stirred it 'til it did appear

To be nearly as light as a spar.

The crew was quite eager to try out the stew.

It tasted so much like fresh chicken!

But the meat was too ripe, and they little knew

From this meal they would likely soon sicken!

The small crew was sated and ready to start

On their mission, though it was dark.

They walked on and on, still quite strong of heart,

Seeking even the spoor of a Snark.

Fit VII
The Boots Meets the Viper

The Boots Meets the Viper

The Boots was a tough lad, well-muscled and strong.
    He sported a grizzled brown beard.
Observant and careful as he marched along,
    Except when the viper appeared!

It was a Gaboon, the most deadly of snakes,
    Not one to be stepped on, for sure.
It bit his thick shin; not much venom it takes
    To fell a strong man, with no cure.

The poison coursed through him and spread all

around.

It went to his gizzard and brain.

He stumbled and wavered, and fell to the ground,

All efforts to help him in vain.

The Boots, soon deceased, was packed back to base.

The Butcher was ready, with snails.

He carved the Boots up into stew meat, apace,

And cooked him, by roasting, in pails.

He added some ginger, some mustard, and rice,

Some brandy (the fat it will render).

It cooked and it simmered (with no added spice).

Finally, that Boots-meat was tender.

The Bellman and Butcher enjoyed the Boots-stew.

(The Beaver ate veggies: a beet.)

The meal was still hot, so on it they blew.

Then devoured most all of the meat.

The Bellman, the Butcher (and Beaver, of course),

Still hunted for wiley old Snark.

They walked a long way, for they had not a horse.

They kept going until it got dark.

Fit VIII
The Butcher Overeats

The Butcher Overeats

The butcher fell ill a day later (his tum!).

    Too much of his own poor cooking!

With pains in his belly and boils on his bum,

    Quite eerily bad he was looking.

He lingered for weeks, getting worse day by day.

    He continued to writhe and decline.

'Twas a pity to see him just wasting away.

    He expired, with no sound nor sign.

The Bellman, appalled, had to deal with the smell.

He dismantled the corpse in five pans.

He boiled it with mushrooms and salted it well,

And put it in forty-two cans.

Along with the tins of the Barrister-meat,

Bellman hid it all under a log,

To save it for later. It would be a treat,

When hungry and cold, in a fog.

The Beaver and Bellman, completely bereft,

Still hunted for Snarks in all weather.

But it seemed, in these woods, that none was still left.

They saw not a claw, nor a feather.

The Beaver's lace-making, a joke as they'd left,

    Was an asset, the way things progressed:

He'd woven a piece with plenty of heft,

    A Snark-net, to catch that big pest!

Many weeks passed, with no sign of a Snark.

    The Bellman ate Barrister's meat;

The Beaver chose tree leaves, and lilies, and bark.

    Strange fruits, they both thought were a treat.

Fit IX
The Bellman Finally
Encounters a Snark

The Bellman Finally Encounters a Snark

The Beaver decided to make his own way.
    He'd build a nice dam on a lake,
A strongly-built lodge, to keep Snarks at bay.
    A fine beaver homestead he'd make.

This plan left the Bellman alone, in the lurch,
    The Snark-net he held in his hand.
He marched on ahead, past fig trees and birch,
    No Snarks to be seen in the land.

With his assigned mission, the Bellman was one.

But suddenly, something arose!

It was scary and massive; weighed more than a ton!

Feathers, claws, and a beak, not a nose!

Its eyes of pale blue had a curious gleam.

The thing was unwilling to move.

The net that the Bellman had tossed was abeam

The Snark, in a bony groove.

The Snark quickly pulled off the net from its head.

The Bellman began to orate.

The Snark snapped him in half, which left him quite
dead.

Both halves were completely insensate.

That Snark was a Boojum, it's sad to relate.

    The Bellman knew not what we do:

The gene that can tell us, before it's too late

    If the thing is a Snark or a Boo—.

On gene forty-two, blue eyes are encoded

    Among other traits most pernicious.

We know what that Snark's eyes, alas, had foreboded.

    Avoid blue-eyed Snarks, as they're vicious!

Epilogue

Epilogue

The Boojum discovered the tinned, preserved meat
    Of the other crew members' remains.
He ate the whole cache, as a wonderful treat.
    But soon rued it: he got some strong pains.

His strong stomach acid, no match for each can,
    Collected inside, at his core.
He'd turned bilious green, like stale marzipan.
    His feathers, he groomed them no more.

The cans of pâté on which he was slumming

Were almost entirely intact.

They'd clogged up the Boojum's own personal plumbing

With oxides (corrosion, in fact).

The Boojum's dilemma could have been fixed,

The ailment that vexed him so cruelly.

Ingesting more tins of old meat should be nixed,

And he needed an enema, truly!

In just a few days, the awful thing died.

He'd rotted away, with much gore.

Resorbed by the forest, including his hide,

He'd frighten no one, any more.

Postscript
The Moral of the Story

The Moral of the Story

What do we need with fine chefs and their books?
 We don't need Rombauer or Child!
We don't need a Crocker or Beeton, for looks,
 When we pine for roast flesh in the wild!

We simply proceed with the corpse that we find,
 And do with it all that we can.
We cut it up, spice it; remove all the rind,
 And fry it all up in a pan!

Snarkasbord Notes

ON THE TEXT

BY

AUGUST A. IMHOLTZ, JR

ON THE ILLUSTRATIONS

BY

ALISON TANNENBAUM

Snarkasbord Notes

FIT THE FIRST:
THE THREAT OF FAMINE

Stanza 1, line 1: The first stanza is almost identical with stanza 13 of "The Bellman's Speech" in the Second Fit of Lewis Carroll's *The Hunting of the Snark*. Lewis Carroll sometimes did borrow from himself but never without a check. Here the word "snark" is written without a capital "S"—a serious failing and a small piece of evidence, i.e. lack of checking, regarding the disputed matter of the true authorship of *Snarkasbord*.

Stanza 1, line 4: "His Boojum"—the pronoun gives an early, almost supernatural, dimension to Carroll's original poem as well as to this sad excuse for an epyllion. Does the author intend the reader to think of a Boojum as a kind of guardian angel in reverse, the technical theological term for which is, pace Karl Barth, "dysangelion" (see Clement of Alexandria, *Stromata* IV.23.42), or is something else at play, however sinister, in this statement?

Illustration to Fit the First: The Bellman at the empty camp dining table. The Snark hunters' store of food has been depleted to the point that even the opportunistic rat (*Rattus norvegicus*) cannot find a scrap to eat. Not even the *Heliconia* plants behind the Bellman are edible. Unless another source of food can be found soon, the threat of famine looms...

Stanza 5, line 3: "would lave"—the assumption here is twofold: first, that Snarks, like cats, penguins, and female high fashion runway models, take extreme pains with self-grooming and individual cleanliness; second, that were it not to be washed (and thus, cleaned of surface bacteria), it would decay rapidly and implode and explode, or vice versa. The subsequent dispersal and natural degradation of the rotten matter would account for the almost total absence of Snark skin, skeleton, DNA, etc. in the zoological collections of the world's museums and laboratories. The hard scientific traces of Sasquatch are equally missing.

Stanza 6, line 1: "map"—presumably a "chart" rather than a map. Carroll makes the same mistake in his poem so perhaps the author of *Snarkasbord* is simply imitating Carroll, if Carroll indeed is not the author.

Stanza 7, line 2: "bagel"—is it strange that there is no reference to bagels in *The Hunting of the Snark* or any other work by Carroll, including his diary entries (see Edward Wakeling, *The Diaries of Lewis Carroll*. Vol. 10. Clifford, Herefordshire: The Lewis Carroll Society, 2007) and his surviving correspondence (see Morton N. Cohen, *The Letters of Lewis Carroll*. New York: Oxford University Press, 1979)? Perhaps this was because bagels were not officially introduced into the Christ Church buttery until 1947. See J.A.R. Mason, *The History of High Table at Oxford, with Particular Reference to the Protocols and Customs of Christ Church*; Oxford: Oxford University Press, 1972. pp. 242-244. The fact that "bagels" is an anagram of "gables" is scarcely worth mentioning.:

Stanza 11, line 4: "prime"—the use of prime here is neither trite nor absurd (admittedly a rarity in this work) but rather a hint about the search for prime numbers, one of the many underlying themes in the quintessential quest saga like *The Hunting of the Snark* and, of course, *Snarkasbord*. Furthermore, another question to be answered is who the prime suspect will be in this tale.

FIT THE SECOND:
THE BILLIARD-MARKER
AND THE BOAR PIT

Stanza 1, line 2: Billiard-Marker—as "the Annotator" observed, "a 'billiard-marker' is the employee of a billiard parlour who keeps a record of the game by marking the points made by each player."

(*The Annotated Hunting of the Snark. The Definitive Edition*. New York: W.W. Norton and Company, 2006. p. 18.) It is perhaps possible that Carroll, if we assume his authorship of this work, learned of Leo Tolstoy's 1855 short story "Notes of a Billiard-Marker" (Записки маркера) during his trip to Russia in 1867 with the Rev. Henry Parry Liddon. That early Tolstoy short story is a study in moral degeneration through addiction to gambling. Whether the present Billiard-Marker followed suit, so to say, is impossible to know.

Despite his pamphlet titled "The Science of Betting," the rumour that Lewis Carroll turned a profit of 42,000 by wagering on horse races at Ascot has no foundation. See Edward Waxwing, "Lewis Carroll and the Silver Blaze: All Bets Are Off" in *A Concise Critique of the Fallacies Surrounding the Life of the Rev. Charles L. Dodgson and His Family* (Clifford: Black Stone Press, 2001).

Stanza 1, line 3: trap for wild boars—this refers to a "pit trap," one of the oldest forms of animal traps known to man, in which sharpened stakes are buried in a pit that is then covered with a thin layer of straw or other camouflage material unable to bear the weight of the animal [or crewmember] attempting to walk across it. Consider the following citations from *The Oxford English Dictionary*:

> 1751. R. Morris *Narr. Life & Astonishing Adventures John Daniel* p. v, Discover they are on an island. Know not what part of the world they are in. Set their pit trap. Catch a calf.
> 1895. R. Kipling *Second Jungle Bk.* 20 It was a pointed stick, such as they set in the mouth of a pit-trap.

Stanza 2, line 3: rice—presumably Basmati rice which is still found today on Snark Island in the better restaurant. The word is from Hindi *bāsmatī*, meaning "fragrant." This would have been of some convenience for those crew members with sensitive noses.

Illustration to Fit the Second: The Billiard-Marker falls into a boring boar trap, losing his walking stick and pipe, and looking quite surprised. The wild boar (*Sus scrofa*), lurking amongst the palmettos (*Sabal palmetto*), looks on with relief at his own narrow escape!

Stanza 3, line 2: fish sauce—this may refer to "garum" (see August Imholtz and Alison Tannenbaum, *Alice Eats Wonderland: An Irreverent Cookbook Adventure*. Carlisle, Massachusetts: Applewood Books, 2009. p. 136.)

Stanza 4, line 4: stew—an old word and an old world cooking word ME *stuwe*, (?) *stuy*, ME—16 *stewe, stue*, ME *stiewe, stwe, styuye, stywe, stywye*, ME—*stew*.

Stew refers to "a preparation of meat slowly boiled in a stew-pan, generally containing vegetables, rice, etc." One almost wonders whether Charles Dickens somehow anticipated *Snarkasbord* when in 1859 he wrote in a *Tale of Two Cities* (ii.iv.51) of "The last sediment of the human stew that had been boiling there all day."

Stanza 5, line 1: Beaver—it is difficult to determine whether this beaver belongs to the species *Castor fiber*, the Eurasian beaver of storied fame, or *Castor canadensis*, the North American beaver featured in Native American and West Virginian folklore down to this day. *Castor Canadensis*, at least, is still famous (or, more correctly, infamous) for continuing to build strong and very effective dams in New England backyards, thereby flooding the owners' properties and making those areas unusable. As a protected species, the offending beavers, much to the property owners' exasperation, cannot be evicted from these areas.

Stanza 5, line 2: kale—a delicacy which has long been the unofficial state vegetable of West Virginia. (West Virginia Legislature. House Joint Resolution 42, 29 January 1903)

Stanza 6, line 4: tall larch—a poor choice of phrase, almost pleonastic in fact, by our otherwise careful author, since all larches grow tall.

Etymology: German *lärche* < Middle High German *lerche, larche* < Old High German **lerihha, *larihha*, an early adoption (prior to the assibilation of *c* in Latin) of Latin *laricem, larix* (whence late Greek λάριξ): corresponding phonetically to Old Celtic **darik-* —and so on ad nauseam for those interested in such arcana.

Presumably our author really means to refer to the coniferous European larch tree, *Larix decidua*.

Stanza 7, line 2: pinot noir—the term for wine from the pinot grape.

Etymology: < French *Pinot* kind of vine (1611 in Cotgrave; late 14th cent. in Middle French as *pynos* (plural), denoting the grapes), spec. a kind of Burgundian vine (1870) < *pin* PINE N.2 + *-ot* -OT SUFFIX, so called on account of the grape cluster resembling a pine cone. Perhaps compare (with different suffix) post-classical Latin *pignolus* kind of vine (1303 in a north Italian source). Compare earlier PINEAU N. (and the etymological note at that entry). (www.oed.com)

The following learned folk etymology from Dickens is unfortunately as wrong as most such etymologies prove to be:

> 1854 *Household. Words* 11 Nov. 310/2 The first and highest in excellence is the Pineau, or Pinot, names guessed to be derived from *nιvω*, I drink.

In the names of particular varieties of vine of the Pinot family, the grape they produce, or the wines made from them. The chief varieties are *Pinot Noir* (in Italy Pinot Nero), used chiefly to make red Burgundy and Champagne; Pinot Gris (in Italy *Pinot Grigio*), from which white wine is made; and Pinot Blanc (in Italy *Pinot Bianco*), a white mutation of *Pinot Gris* first observed in Burgundy at the end of the 19th cent. (www.oed.com) *Pinot Noir*, of course, is not to be confused with *Pinot Sour* of West Virginia.

Stanza 7, line 4: steak tartare—"a dish usually consisting of raw minced beefsteak mixed with egg and seasonings". It can prove lethal when consumed in large quantities, especially in warm climates like Snark Island. Some believe the dish is named after "sauce tartare" a mayonnaise-based concoction with white vinegar, capers, and—at one's discretion—green lizard eggs. It has nothing to do with the nomadic Tartar peoples who would never have eaten such a sissy dish anyway.

Fit the Third:
The Banker and the Cliff

Stanza 1, line 1: traipsing—to traipse— to walk or travel about without apparent plan, with or without a purpose. Suitable as the word may be here, its origin, not surprisingly, is unknown. In an obscure 18th century edition of the Greek text of Hesiod's *Theogony,* however, we do find at I.78, a contested conjectural reading of "Traipsichore" for "Terpsichore" though the meter would scarcely admit it—see Thomas Cooke, *Hesiod* (Cambridge: Cambridge University Press, 1756) p. 42.

Stanza 1, line 4: second-hand note—a banking term having several meanings. Basically, a second-hand note is the opposite of a first-hand note. First, its currency sense may be clear from the following.

Henry Clifford Stuart in his outrageous book *Principally about Finance* (Washington, DC: Judd and Detweiler, 1911) noted:

"The turning in for redemption of that funny part of our present currency which is based upon government bonds, will not increase the debt balance of the government at all, but it will make a decided change in the holding of the creditor, who will have the bond itself as security instead of second-hand notes as at present. The only apparent loss will be in the redemption of the gold and silver, which childhood's toys our governmental parent must take off our hands." (p. 86)

From the U.S. Federal Reserve report *The Use and counterfeiting of United states Currency abroad. A Report to the Congress by the Secretary of the Treasury in Consultation with the Advanced Counterfeit Deterrence Steering Committee, Pursuant to Section 807 of PL 104-32* here is the other sense of "second-hand notes":

In view of the disadvantages in handling used currency, not all of the U.S. banknote distributors are willing to deal with second-hand notes. Those that are have created a 'redirect market' for them, but even then only the higher quality used notes are deemed acceptable. While not a great deal of information is available…it appears that the primary economic justification for dealing only with new notes is to avoid the sizeable costs incurred in fitness sorting and authentication of used notes."

Stanza 2, line 4: packed him with frogs—a primitive though effective short-term alternative when ice is in limited supply as it often is, for example, in the Amazon jungle and on Snark Island. It is not advisable to attempt to use toads for this purpose, however cool they may feel.

Illustration to Fit the Third: The Banker, having stumbled, falls off the cliff, landing heavily between the patches of cacti at the bottom. The placid iguana (*Iguana iguana*), although rudely interrupted in feeding on his favourite yellow *Brachycereus* flowers, seems unconcerned.

Stanza 3, line 2: mango—The mango is a fleshy stone fruit belonging to the genus *Mangifera*, consisting of numerous tropical fruiting trees in the flowering plant family Anacardiaceae. (This family also includes poison ivy. Those sensitive to the irritant urushiol in poison ivy may experience an unpleasant tingling or itching of the lips on ingesting mango). The mango is native to India from where it spread all over the world including, of course, Snark Island. This "mango" is not to be confused with the wildly popular Japanese comic book genre that has spread like oriental jam across the face of America.

The English word "mango" originated from the Tamil word *mānkay* (மாங்காய்) or the Malayalam word *mānna* (മാങ്ങ; from the Dravidian root word for the same), via Portuguese (also *manga*). The word's first recorded attestation in a European language was a text by Ludovico di Varthema in Italian in 1510, as *manga*; the first recorded occurrences in languages such as French and post-classical Latin appear to be the translations from this Italian text. The origin of the "-o" ending in English is unclear as you may well understand. (www.oed.com)

Stanza 3, line 3: gar—the name gar (or garpike) is strictly applied to members of the *Lepisosteidae*, a family including seven living species of fish in two genera that inhabit fresh, brackish, and occasionally marine, waters of eastern Snark Island.

The word probably derives from *gar* meaning "spear" *Belone belone* is now more commonly referred to as the "garfish" or "gar fish" to avoid confusion with the North American gars of the family *Lepisosteidae*. Confusingly, the name "garfish" is commonly used for a number of other species of the related genera Strongylura, Tylosurus and Xenentodon of the family *Belonidae* as well as of some more distantly related genera in the suborder *Belonoidei*. (www.oed.com)

Attempts to establish any relation between "gar" and "garbage" are quite wrong-headed.

Furthermore, there is no proof, despite persistent rumors along the Texas Gulf Coast, that a saltwater gar has ever eaten any of the bathers foolish enough to swim in Galveston Bay.

Stanza 4, line 1: forty-two—the number 42 figures in Carroll's *The Hunting of the Snark* and it was, Carroll himself admitted, a number with which he was fascinated in his real life. Much has been written about the significance of 42. "The Annotator" in Note 34 of his *The Annotated Hunting of the Snark, The Definitive Edition* (New York: W.W. Norton & Co., 2006) presents several permutations on the possible significance of the number 42 in the *The Hunting of the Snark*. The most thorough treatment of 42, however, may well be Edward Wakeling's essay "What I Tell You Forty-Two Times Is

True" in *Jabberwocky*, vol. 6, No. 4, Autumn 1977, pp. 101-106. Both "The Commentator" and Wakeling, nonetheless, fail to note that none of the members of the crew, not even the esteemed Beaver, have 42 chromosomes, a distinction accruing only to the wolverine, the rhesus monkey, the rat, and the rhea, an the Asian "raccoon dog", none of which, unfortunately was able to weasel its way into the expedition.

Tove Jansson, the famous Finnish illustrator of things Moomin, curiously depicts 44 boxes, not the traditional 42, abandoned on the beach (Tate Publishing, 2011, p. [16]).

FIT THE FOURTH: THE BONNET-MAKER IN THE MANGROVES

Stanza 1, line 1: Bonnet-maker—surely the most miscast member of the crew, for there is no one who needs or would wear a bonnet, especially during a Snark hunt, for it is common knowledge that Snarks cannot abide the sight of them. In a 1992 essay in *Jabberwocky, the Journal of the Lewis Carroll Society*, Gregory Ackland and Gabriel Ackland had argued that in Lewis Carroll's Snark poem there is really no crew member named the "Bonnet-maker" for they understand the phrase to be in apposition to "the Boots." The verses read:

> The crew was complete: it included a Boots—
> A maker of Bonnets and Hoods—
> A Barrister ...

As "the Annotator" noted (p. 17), the Acklands "make no comment on Holiday's picture of the Bonnet-maker holding a lady's bonnet." However, there is another sense of "bonnet" which may have some relevance at least for the verses under consideration here. Bonnet, A weel or snare for fish. *Obs.*1715 tr. G. Pancirolli *Hist. Mem. Things* I. i. i. 5 They cast abundance of them [Shell-fish] into the Sea, in Weels or Bonnets for that purpose.

Stanza 1, line 4: skate—here our author refers to a fish of the genus *Raia*; esp. the common species *Raia batis*, a very large, flat, cartilaginous fish much used for food and in some cultures moccasin insoles. Etymology: < Old Norse *skata* (still in Norwegian and Icelandic use; Faroese *sköta*). 1. A fish of the genus *Raia*; esp. the common species *Raia batis*, a very large, flat, cartilaginous fish much used for food. (www.oed.com)

Stanza 2, line 2: hams—ham may refer either to buttock with its associated thigh—usually used in plural; or to a cut of meat consisting of a thigh; especially one from a hog. Another sense, which could have offered some confusion, is that a skate's hams were called rumples [see the famous 1823 usage by Sir Walter Scott *St Ronan's Well*, I. iii. 64 [An] "auld fule..., that may hae some judgment in cock-bree or in scate-rumples".

Illustration to Fit the Fourth: The Bonnet-Maker sinks into the red mangrove (*Rhizophora mangle*) swamp. He grasps at a nearby leafy twig, but fails to reach it. Alas, one of his more elaborate bonnets gets ruined in the brackish water, and the roseate spoonbill (*Ajaja ajaja*) wonders whether some of those colourful ribbons would nicely adorn its nest...

Stanza 3, line 4: bœuf bourguignon—simply beef braised with red wine and served with bacon and mushrooms as prepared in the eponymous region of France more famous for its truffles than its cattle. The dish was popularized in the United States by Julia Child. (For Julia's own deliciously succulent Beef Bourguignon recipe please see abcnews.go.com/GMA/recipe?id=8222804.

Stanza 4, line 1: fresh pork—on first consideration a very strange remark about bœuf bourguignon, since not even the most frenchified beef ever really tastes like pork. Perhaps this means the crew are beginning to suffer from dysgeusia, a sometimes severe distortion of the sense of taste usually related, quite surprisingly, to fast food consumption (see the 2003 exhaustive study in *The Lancet*, "Hooked on carbs: fast food linked to dysgeusia and consequent dopamine deprivation" by O'Connor, Dematikos, Shapiro, Pritchards, and Gonzales, Vol. 362, No. 93780, pp. 602–603). Or perhaps a simpler explanation may be that the memory of the bacon in the bœuf bourguignon was too overpowering for the beef flavour to linger in their minds Madeleine-fashion!

FIT THE FIFTH:
THE BARRISTER FINDS HONEY

Stanza 1, line 2: Barrister—a rumpoled figure differing from a solicitor in several ways, although both are given to sporting bowler hats.

"Barristers specialise in courtroom advocacy, drafting legal pleadings and giving expert legal opinions. They can be contrasted with solicitors—the other class of lawyer in split professions—who have more direct access with clients, and may do transactional-type legal work. Barristers are rarely hired by clients directly but instead are retained (or instructed) by solicitors to act on behalf of clients."

(en.wikipedia.org/wiki/Barrister)

Barristers, in addition to wearing Bowler—always black, never green— hats outside the court, usually wear a horsehair wig, stiff collar, bands and a gown in court; although our Barrister on Snark Island now has no use for such accoutrements.

Stanza 1, line 3: honey—fructose and glucose which share the "common chemical formula $C_6H_{12}O_6$. They differ not only in their linear forms but also in their cyclization products: D-Glucose in its linear form reacts to yield the cyclic hemiacetyl alpha-D-glucopyranose, and D-Fructose in its linear form reacts to yield the hemiketal alpha-D-fructofuranose."

(answers.yahoo.com/question/index?qid=20071231235741AA4rbBE)

Stanza 1, line 4: stung—bee stings can cause anaphylactic shock resulting, as in this case, in death.

Anaphylaxis is defined as "a serious allergic reaction that is rapid in onset and may cause death". It can result in a number of different symptoms including throat swelling, an itchy rash, and low blood pressure. On a pathophysiologic level it is an acute multi-system type I hypersensitivity reaction. The term comes from the Greek words ανά ana, *against*, and φύλαξις phylaxis, *protection*.

Stanza 2, line 3: first aid—Recommended medical assistance for first-aid for bee stings consists of the following, according to Wikipedia:

"Anaphylaxis is a medical emergency that may require resuscitation measures such as airway management, supplemental oxygen, large volumes of intravenous fluids, and close monitoring.

Administration of epinephrine is the treatment of choice with antihistamines and steroids often used as adjuncts. A period of in hospital observation for between 6 and 24 hours is recommended for people once they have returned to normal due to concerns of biphasic anaphylaxis" (en.wikipedia.org/wiki/Anaphylaxis). Clearly, these life-saving medical measures were not available on Snark Island.

Illustration to Fit the Fifth: The Barrister encounters a tree nest of Africanized honeybees (*Apis mellifera* x) in a lovely tropical glade, complete with blooming bromeliad (genus and species unknown), palm leaves, and a vigorous strangler fig (*Ficus aurea*) climbing the petticoat palm (*Washingtonia robusta*) trunk. Still dressed neatly in his court finery, the Barrister tries to figure out how to acquire the honey that must surely be inside the hostile hive. Alas, the killer bees are about to attack him, and the cockatoo (*Cacatua* sp.), who might have voiced a caution, appears indifferent to the Barrister's impending plight.

Stanza 3, line 2: swamp gas –swamp gas is "produced by the anaerobic digestion or fermentation of biodegradable materials such as biomass, manure, sewage, municipal waste, green waste, plant material, and crops. Biogas comprises primarily methane (CH_4) and carbon dioxide (CO_2) and may have small amounts of hydrogen sulphide (H_2S) (the source of the unpleasant odor), moisture and siloxanes." (en.wikipedia.org/wiki/Swamp_gas) All three are serious contributors to global warming, and according to Al Gore, threaten the inhabitability of Snark Island. He recommends that everyone should immediately stop eating and breathing. For goodness sakes, think of the Snarks!

Stanza 4, line 2: blimp-like—first a note on blimp: From the redoubtable Wikipedia again we learn that: "The term "blimp" is reportedly onomatopoeic, the sound the airship makes when one taps the envelope (balloon) with a finger. Although there is some disagreement among historians, credit for coining the term is usually given to Lt. A. D. Conningham of the British Royal Navy in 1915.

A 1943 etymology published in the *New York Times* supports the British origin of the word: during the First World War when the British were experimenting with lighter-than-air craft. The initial non-rigid aircraft was called the A-limp; and a second version called the B-limp was deemed more satisfactory.

(en.wikipedia.org/wiki/Blimp)

A different derivation is given by Barnes & James in *Shorts Aircraft since 1900*:

> "In February 1915 the need for anti-submarine patrol airships became urgent, and the Submarine Scout type was quickly improvised by hanging an obsolete B.E.2c fuselage from a spare Willows envelope; this was done by the R.N.A.S. at Kingsnorth, and on seeing the result for the first time, Horace Short, already noted for his very apt and original vocabulary, named it "Blimp", adding, "What else would you call it?"
>
> (en.wikipedia.org/wiki/Blimp)

Stanza 4, line 2: the corpse: As to how the body swells, Wiki Answers answers:

> "The human body is basically made of organic materials like carbohydrates which when decompose will break up into CO_2 (carbon dioxide) and H_2O (water). As we all know, when the state of a material changes from either solid or liquid to gas the volume of the material increases. Due to this change of state and with no way for the gases to escape, the dead body swells. In due course of time, the gas builds up pressure throughout the bodily tissues. During this process, fluids are forced to escape from natural orifices, such as the nose, mouth, and anus, and enter the surrounding environment. The build up of pressure may also cause rupturing of the skin.
>
> (wiki.answers.com/Q/Why_do_dead_bodies_swell_up)

Stanza 4, line 4: stooge—presumably in the fourth sense of the word meaning a lackey, though this may have been somewhat prejudicial of our Barrister. The OED admits the origin of the word is unclear: "Origin unknown; the possibility that it represents an altered form of *student* has been suggested." (www.oed.com) However, those familiar with the activities of "The Three Stooges" (Moe, Larry, and Curly) will know exactly what is meant by "stooge."

Stanza 5, line 2: pampas-grass—the allegedly edible hedge *Cortaderia selloana*. The authors do not recommend making a meal of this coarse, tasteless, fibre.

Stanza 6, line 3: pâté—spread of finely chopped or puréed seasoned meat, from the French word for paste, which it often resembles. Pâté is usually prepared with a high proportion of fat from the same animal that provided the meat.

FIT THE SIXTH:
THE BROKER ENCOUNTERS
THE TOAD

Stanza 1, line 1: Broker—again "The Annotator" succinctly described this crew member as: "not a pawnbroker, but one licensed to appraise and sell household goods. When a landlord took possession of the furniture of those unable to pay rent, the broker would be called in to 'value their goods'." (*The Annotated Hunting of the Snark, The Definitive Edition* (New York: W.W. Norton & Co., 2006. P. 17) What value a Broker could possibly place on a Snark or its possessions (which would be what? Bathing machines?) is unknown.

Stanza 1, line 2: toad—very likely the very poisonous "Cane Toad" or *Bufo marinus*, a member of the subgenus Rhinella of the genus Bufo, which has been introduced to many regions of the Pacific as well as on Snark Island. (en.wikipedia.org/wiki/Cane_toad)

Stanza 1, line 3: forbode—"to have an inward conviction of"—a nearly obsolete use but one that fits the rhyme.

Stanza 1, line 4: bufagins—the technical term, or terminus technicus as some snobs would insist, for toad poisons. More precisely, the toxins are toxic steroids whose effects are similar to digitalis poisoning. Some bufagins are known to be employed, in discrete dosages of course, in traditional Chinese medicine and in some TexMex taco salsas.

Stanza 2, line 4: unable to talk—a telltale effect of bufagin poisoning not dissimilar to the effects of overindulgence in tacos and margaritas.

Illustration to Fit the Sixth: The Broker, walking through a healthy stand of sugarcane (*Saccharum edule*), cannot resist the idea of picking up the large, pudgy specimen of *Bufo marinus* for a closer look. The Beaver (*Castor fiber*), familiar with the effects of bufagens on mammals, looks on in dismay, but cannot dissuade the Broker.

Stanza 3, line 2: under his nose—the "philtrum" is the area below the base of the nose and the top of the upper lip. It is one of the most ticklish places on the human body, especially one with a moustache.

Stanza 4. line 4: apace—that is "swiftly' which was necessary because the bufagin poison would have spread throughout the body before the onset of rigour, which in Snark climates occurs with unusual rapidity.

Stanza 5, line 2: guar—the guar bean or so-called cluster bean (*Cyamopsis tetragonoloba*) is an annual legume and the source of guar gum. It grows best under conditions with frequent rainfall, but tolerates arid conditions well. About 80% of world production occurs in India, but, due to strong demand, the plant is being introduced into new areas. It is known as *gawaar* in Hindi and Marathi, *goruchikkudu kaya*. Guar gum is used in dairy products like ice cream and as a stabilizer in cheese and cold-meat processing (en.wikipedia.org/wiki/Guar)—for which it has a real use in cases like that of the Broker.

Stanza 5, line 4: spar—a light pole used in the rigging of a ship. Booms, not those one hears in the night, and masts, are common examples of spars on sailing ships.

Stanza 6, line 2: fresh chicken—reliable reports have challenged the long-held view that human flesh tastes more like chicken than, say, okra, salmon, or even pork.

The 16 October 2007 issue of the German news magazine *Der Spiegel* published an interview, which begins with this statement: "Armin Meiwes, the German cannibal serving a life sentence for killing and eating a man who begged to be devoured, has described how the meat tasted of pork and how he prepared an elaborate meal of human steak in a green pepper sauce with croquettes and Brussels sprouts."

(www.spiegel.de/international/zeitgeist/ 0,1518,511775,00.html)

Zhu-Can, a rebel leader of an agrarian army during the end of the Sui Dynasty in early seventh-century China, was an extremely cruel warlord who was much addicted to cannibalism. He is said to have encouraged his soldiers to eat women and infants, stating, "Human flesh is the most delicious flesh. As long as there are people around, we need not worry about hunger." (en.wikipedia.org/wiki/ Zhu_Can) The folk association of Zhu-Can with canned goods, especially canned chicken or pork for that matter, is utterly groundless.

Fit the Seventh:
The Boots Meets the Viper

Stanza 1, line 1: Boots—a "boots" to quote "the Annotator" again, is "a servant at a hotel or inn, formerly assigned to such low tasks as cleaning boots and brushing clothes." (*The Annotated Hunting of the Snark, The Definitive Edition* (New York: W. W. Norton & Co., 2006. P. 17) Usually he is very much of a below-stairs sort, but the Boots chosen by the Bellman was in fact a graduate of Clare College, Cambridge, and Senior Wrangler, who had fallen on hard times because of his obsession with Fibonacci numbers and his attempts to find their patterns in boot laces and other man-made as well as natural things.

Stanza 2, line 1: Gaboon—the Gaboon adder, also Gaboon viper (tr. French *échidnée du Gabon* (Duméril & Bibron, in *Erpétologie générale* (1854) VII. 1428)) is the poisonous snake, *Bitis gabonica*. Named from the African country where it is most often but not exclusively found. "*Bitis gabonica* has the longest fangs and the highest venom yield of any venomous snake in the world." (goafrica.about.com/od/africasafariguide/tp/Africansnakes.html)

Stanza 2, line 3: venom—the "Gaboon viper venom contains two proteins, known as *hemorrhagins*, that cause blood vessels to spill their contents into the surrounding tissues. These large proteins diffuse slowly through the bloodstream, resulting in severe pain, intensive swelling and oozing of blood from the site of the bite. But eventually the proteins find their way to distant parts of the body, where they cause spontaneous hemorrhages in major organs. Death is usually due to heart failure." (animal.discovery.com/tv/wild-recon/science-of-venom/ gaboon-viper-venom.html)

See also "Effect of gaboon viper (*Bitis gabonica*) venom on blood coagulation, platelets, and the fibrinolytic enzyme system" by C. D. Forbes, A. G. G. Turpie, J. C. Ferguson, G. P. McNicol, and A. S. Douglas, *Journal of Clinical Pathology*, 1969 May; 22(3): 312–316.

Illustration to Fit the Seventh: The Boots, traipsing along a forest path lined with a lush patch of Flame Violets (*Episcia dianthiflora*), unwittingly approaches the viper. While busily admiring the large and striking-looking Brazilian owl-faced moth (*Caligo eurilochus* *brasiliensis*) perched on the *Episcia* leaves, the Boots accidentally steps right onto the deadly Gaboon Viper (*Bitis gabonica*).

Stanza 3, line 2: gizzard and brain—in most Boots these organs have much in common.

Stanza 4, line 2: snails—presumably *Helix pomatia*, the Burgundy snail, Roman snail, and on some menus Escargot. Ironically, often a favourite pub food of the Boots, whose shell striated patterns he would analyse for hours on end.

Stanza 5, line 4: tender—as in the phrase "tender as shoe leather"

FIT THE EIGHTH:
THE BUTCHER OVEREATS

Stanza 1, line 3: boils—*Hidradenitis suppurativa*, which according to the account provided by the Mayo Clinic, is "a severe form of acne (acne inversa), which occurs deep in the skin around oil (sebaceous) glands and hair follicles. The parts of the body affected—the groin and armpits, for example—are also the main locations of apocrine sweat glands." Boils are especially common in butchers and Central European traditional cooks who work regularly with lard. See the Mayo Clinic site:

(www.mayoclinic.com/health/hidradenitis-suppurativa/DS00818)

Illustration to Fit the Eighth: The Bellman in the process of canning the Barrister-meat. Obviously, the Bellman has become very efficient at this; he is a one-man assembly line as he cooks the meat and fills the tins with it. He works so efficiently that the optimistic hyena (*Crocuta crocuta*), lurking nearby in the shadow of a poisonous oleander bush (*Nerium oleander*), will probably not get even a taste of the delicious concoction. Fortunately the Bellman was familiar with the poisonous quality of oleander, and was careful not to get any of the leaves into the meat.

Stanza 3, line 1: smell—the smell is the result of release of a chemical called "putrescine (1,4 diaminobutane $NH_2(CH_2)_4NH_2$), as the name implies, a malodorous organic compound within the polyamine family—a group of molecules already known to play a crucial role in important functions like cell division." In minute quantities it has been found in some French perfumes.

See blogs.discovermagazine.com/discoblog/2011/03/14/ chemical-behind-the-smell-of-rotting-flesh-prevents-seizures-in-tadpoles/

Stanza 3, line 3: mushrooms—which species would have been at hand is difficult to say. *Boletus edulis* or *Cantharellus cibarius* are likely choices though the Bellman may have been partial to the bell mushrooms, especially *Psilocybe semilanceata.*

Stanza 4, line 4: log—presumably the Bellman is recalling fond memories of beef and other jerked logs while aboard ship

Stanza 5, line 2: hunted—their pace must have been severely compromised unless the Bellman carried the Beaver, for which generous gesture there sadly is no evidence.

Stanza 6, line 1: lace making—Beaver lace, as commonly acknowledged, has twice the tensile strength of steel. (See E. Q. Doyle "On the Comparative Properties of Dow Elastomers and Castor lace." *Industrial Yarns*, Vol.24, 1988. pp. 301-309.)

FIT THE NINTH:
THE BELLMAN FINALLY
ENCOUNTERS A SNARK

Stanza 1, line 3: lodge—the den built by beavers. The dry, snug lodge is carefully constructed of tree branches and mud, and is placed in the open water of the beaver pond, which was made by the damming of a small stream of water to flood a meadow. The living quarters of the lodge are above the water line, but the entrances are below the water, to discourage entry by predators (such as Snarks). The winter supply of food (the bark of tree branches and twigs) for the beaver family is stored near the lodge for easy access when the pond is frozen.

It is highly unlikely that a beaver pond on tropical Snark Island would ever freeze over, unless, of course, the Yellowstone caldera erupts once again and triggers the next ice age.

Stanza 1, line 3: Snarks at bay—Snarks are aquaphobic, not hydrophobic which means something quite different, and so the Beaver's Lady of Shalott approach should guarantee her safety. There is some reason to think that the lace-making Beaver is indeed feminine (See Mark Richards "The gender of the Beaver in *The Snark*" *Jabberwocky*, Vol. 14, No. 2, 1985, p. 40; and Alfreda Blanchard "The gender of the Beaver in The Hunting of the Snark and serving the Snark with greens" *Jabberwocky*, Vol. 15, No. 3, 1986, p. 55.

Stanza 2, line 1: lurch—always idiomatically used with the definite rather than indefinite article. The expression comes from a really silly French board game which, not surprisingly, died out in the 17th century. The phrase "left in the lurch" thus originates:

> ... from the French board game of *lourche* or *lurch*, which was similar to backgammon and was last played in the 17th century (the rules having now been lost). Players suffered a lurch if they were left in a hopeless position from which they couldn't win the game. The card game of cribbage, or crib, also has a 'lurch' position which players may be left in if they don't progress half way round the peg board before the winner finishes.

The game came to England from continental Europe and its name derives from the word 'left', which is *lurtsch* in dialect German and *loyrtz* in Middle Dutch.

(www.phrases.org.uk/meanings/left-in-the-lurch.html)

The suggestion that 'lurch' is a simple typographical error for 'lunch' is hotly disputed, in spite of the fact that the phrase "left for lunch" has entered the idiom of many dialects.

Illustration to Fit the Ninth: The Bellman meets his destiny. In a dense forest of Boojum trees (*Idria columnaris*), the Bellman is taken by surprise... Even the gray parrot (*Psittacus erythacus*) has no intention of staying around long enough to find out what is going to happen.

Stanza 3, line 4: not a nose—the absence of which may go some way to account for the Snark's fondness for bathing machines, which often were redolent of more than the tang of the sea.

Stanza 4, line 1: pale blue—a clear attestation of the Snark's Indo-European ancestry. See A. Crane, K. Matsumoto, Y. Bar Elam, and J. Smith "Blue eye colour in snarks may be caused by a perfectly associated founder mutation in a regulatory element located within the *HERC2* gene inhibiting *OCA2* expression" *Studia Snarkiana*, Vol. XLII, No. 7, 1993 p. 21.

Stanza 4, line 4: bony groove—"In all other theropods with the exception of *Avimimus* (ROM 46144) and abelisaurids (MACN CH 894), a well-developed ligament groove that runs obliquely from proximomedially to laterodistally, is present on the posterior side of the femoral head." Oliver W. M. Rauhut. "The Interrelationships and Evolution of Basal Theropod Dinosaurs" *Special Papers in Paleontology*, No. 69. 1969. p. 112.

Stanza 5, line 1: pulled off the net from its head—*de-snooded*, as it were.

Stanza 5, line 2: orate—like King Canute (885-1035), who may have been the Bellman's distant ancestor.

Illustration to Fit the Ninth: As the Bellman suffers his fate, the Jubjub bird (*Jubjub snarkensis*), who happened to be nearby at the time, looks on with concern.

E P I L O G U E

Stanza 1, line 1: Boojum—a species of Snark (*Snarka boojuma*) far more dangerous than the common Snark (*Snarka innocuosa*).

Stanza 2, line 1: stomach acid—or gastric acid is a digestive fluid, formed in the stomach. It has a pH of 1 to 2 [on a logarithmic scale] and is composed of hydrochloric acid (HCl) (around 0.5%, or 5000 parts per million), and large quantities of potassium chloride (KCl) and sodium chloride (NaCl). The acid plays a key role in digestion of proteins, by activating digestive enzymes, and making ingested proteins unravel so that digestive enzymes can break down the long chains of amino acids. (en.wikipedia.org/wiki/Gastric_acid)

Like Coca-Cola, stomach acid can be effective in cleaning the posts of one's automobile battery posts, although it is hard to find in 12-ounce bottles."

Stanza 2, line 2: marzipan—a confection made of egg whites, sugar and ground almonds. It is often shaped and coloured like fresh fruit, in miniature. In its normal state it is stale. The frequent consumption can result in the loss of amalgam fillings.

Stanza 3, line 4: oxides—The oxide ion, O^{2-}, is the conjugate base of the hydroxide ion, OH^-, and is encountered in ionic solid such as calcium oxide. O^{2-} is unstable in aqueous solution − its affinity for H^+ is so great ($pK_b \sim -22$) that it abstracts a proton from a solvent H_2O molecule: $O^{2-} + H_2O \rightarrow 2\ OH^-$ (en.wikipedia.org/wiki/Oxide)

Stanza 5, line 4: frighten no more—like the end of Grendel and numerous other monsters of world literature, there is something strangely poignant about the creature's passing.

POSTSCRIPT:
THE MORAL OF THE STORY

Stanza 1, line 2: Rombauer—Irma Rombauer (1877–1962) author of the popular American cookbook *The Joy of Cooking*. She died from botulism poisoning traced back to her own home-canned parsnips.

Stanza 1, line 2: Child—Julia Child (1912–2004), an American spy, cookbook author, and star of a television cooking show. Her *The Art of Albanian Cooking*, unlike her best-selling *Mastering the Art of French Cooking*, never achieved the popularity it deserved.

Stanza 1, line 3: Crocker—The name was first developed by the Washburn Crosby Company in 1921 as a way to give a personalized response to consumer product questions. The name Betty was selected because it was viewed as a cheery, all-American name. It was paired with the last name Crocker, in honor of William Crocker, a Washburn Crosby Company director.

(en.wikipedia.org/wiki/Betty_Crocker)

Perhaps the origin of the phrase "comes a crocker" is an expression once used at dinner by Henry Cabot Lodge in reference to a dessert obviously having come from a box.

Stanza 1, line 3: Beeton—Isabella Beeton (1836–1865), famous as the author of *Mrs. Beeton's Book of Household Management*—the staple cookbook of the Victorian and Edwardian middle class and some servants in Singapore. At the young age of 28 she perished from overindulgence in Cherry Bakewells which had been prepared, somehow unknowingly, in contravention of her own recipe.

Stanza 2, line 4: pan—rather like a "pan pizza".

A Missing Fit

FROM LEWIS CARROLL'S
THE HUNTING OF THE SNARK

"The Booking"

BY

CHARLIE LOVETT

Introduction

*T*he following unpublished manuscript fragment of Lewis Carroll's great nonsense poem *The Hunting of the Snark* was discovered by the noted Carrollian scholar Edgar Cuthwellis in the papers of the Westhill collection. Cuthwellis conjectures that Dodgson originally intended the fit to precede "Fit the Seventh—The Banker's Fate," and that some of the stanzas might have been intended for "Fit the First—The Landing." Dodgson's decision to excise "The Booking" may have been a result of his desire to keep the meaning of *The Snark* ambiguous. The inclusion of this fit "lets the cat out of the bag" in revealing that the entire poem is an allegory on book collecting. The fragment is published here for the first time.

Charlie Lovett
14 January 1998

The Booking

He sought them with thimbles, he sought them with
care.
He pursued them with forks and hope.
He threatened their lives with a railway share.
He charmed them with smiles and soap.

He was one who, in spite of the cracks in his joints,
And some rather bad wear to his spine,
Was a master of imprints, of bindings and points,
And was often described as "near fine."

He came as a Bookman, but whispered to Boots,

    While shelving octavos astern,

"I prefer 'Bibliographer'—that label suits

    The owner of Keats' Grecian Urn."

He collected rare issues and challenged his wits

    By inspecting each page for small tears.

He was found in pursuit of ephemeral bits

    At the monthly Society Fairs.

He tallied the commas in *Oliver Twist*

    (Four thousand one hundred and eight),

And wrote *Notes and Queries* a piece to assist

    In defining first issue, third state.

He was bound in Morocco from hat to his shoes

With a dust jacket pulled round his chest.

His flyleaves were marbled with yellows and blues.

On his fore-edge was painted a crest.

The Broker, who read *Book Collector* each month

Appraised the new man just by looking,

And said with his lisp, "There is land ahead, onth

We are there, would you care to go booking?"

And when, by the locks of their hair, they reached

land,

The Bookman and Broker set out,

Shepherd's Guide to Snark Island firmly in hand—

An appraiser and literal scout.

At the first stop were Penguins and dreck on display.

    There was rubbish in dusty dark nooks.

Then they bypassed a boot sale and S.P.C.K.

    And happened on Jubjub Rare Books.

The Proprietor eyed them with scrupulous scorn

    From his perch high above bins of prints.

His corners were bumped and his covers were worn,

    And his burblings hardly made sense.

The Bookman and Broker, their hearts filled with
    hope,

    Unfolded their want list with care.

They shook out the forks and they washed off the
    soap,

    And they gazed at the one title there.

"'Tis a tome," said the Bookman, "I've sought all my
  years,
    Through the fog, through the snow, through the
    dark.
I've hunted the forests of five hemispheres
    For the famous 'Incunable Snark.'"

They sorted through fiction—from A down to Zed
    They mined heaps of history and delved
In a dank basement room on a carved wooden bed
    Where rare juvenilia was shelved.

A yellowing pamphlet they found on the floor
    On "The Boojum and Baker Dispute"
They left mouldering there, inclined to ignore
    All volumes outside their pursuit.

The Broker checked costs against price guides and
what

 He knew from his years as a hound.

"Should we meet with a Snark, more likely than not,

 We shall need at least forty-two pound!"

Then the Bookman dashed forward and shouted aloud

 In a voice that was mimsy but pure

"'Tis a Snark bound in vellum I see through the
crowd,

 'Tis a Snark, 'Tis a Snark, I am sure."

The bookshop had somehow quite vanished from sight

 And the Bookman and Broker now stood

In an Auction room raucous with sounds of the fight

 For a manuscript volume of Hood.

"And now lot forty-two," the old auctioneer cried

"Twenty pounds," called the Bookman with glee.

"Thirty pounds, forty pounds," he added with pride,

"Forty-one, forty-two, forty three!"

"I have forty three pounds from the man in the back,

Is there any advance on the sum?"

The room was dead silent, not one snicker-snack,

For the bidders had all been struck dumb.

"Forty-three going once, forty three going twice,"

The Bookman felt ready to roar,

Then a voice from behind him like ashes and ice

Intoned with a growl "Forty-four."

The Bookman searched vainly in waistcoat and shoe

    For a Guinea to give the cashier.

"I would bid sixty-five, I would bid eighty-two,

    If only the Banker were here."

His pockets were empty—not a shilling or crown

    No silver or copper or gold.

He beheld in bleak horror the hammer come down

    And the auctioneer bellow out "Sold!"

The Bookman looked tattered, his margins were

    soiled,

    And foxing appeared on his face.

His chance for a Snark had been fiendishly foiled,

    And he slunk from the room in disgrace.

He read Alfred Lord Tennyson, cited Defoe,

He paraphrased Shakespeare and Burns.

He recited eight stanzas of Edgar A. Poe,

Quoting Wordsworth and Homer in turns.

The Broker's heart broke to observe such despair

As he walked with his friend towards the beach,

And he told the sad story to those who were there

Of the Snark that had been within reach.

The Bookman checked out of the crew on that night

And he never recouped his esprit,

All from having the rare printed Snark in his sight—

The *Ex Libris* that wasn't to be.

Two Missing Fits

FROM LEWIS CARROLL'S
THE HUNTING OF THE SNARK

"The Recrewting"

AND

"The Sailing"

BY

CHARLIE LOVETT

Introduction

*I*n 1998, I presented the results of my research into missing fits of Lewis Carroll's epic nonsense poem, *The Hunting of the Snark*. At that time, based on the evidence that was then available to me from the Westhill collection and its curator Edgar Cuthwellis, I assumed that the verses which I read to you had been cut from the original poem, partly at the behest of Henry Holiday, the illustrator. The publication of the missing fit which I presented, "The Booking," was met with resounding silence from critics and literary scholars around the globe, and it is without modesty that I claim that my publishing those verses was one of the most insignificant literary events of the Dodgson centenary year. Since that time, as you all certainly know, Mr. Cuthwellis has chosen to deny any relation to or knowledge of the Westhill collection, and he returns all inquiries marked "Addressee Unknown". It is my understanding that he has even printed up a circular letter denying that he is Edgar Cuthwellis, though this piece is quite rare and I have not yet had the opportunity to inspect a copy. Last month, I took matters into my own hands and travelled to the Westhill collection where I was permitted into the reading room under the name Mr. Dares (that is to say, the name Mr. Dares was written over the door, and I entered the room under it).

Imagine my shock when, after several days of sifting through boxes of uncatalogued manuscript material, I discovered that "The Booking," was not the only unpublished fit of the *Snark* in the collection. Though I did not have sufficient time to sort through all the material in the several boxes of papers that were presented to me, I did discover two additional fits, published here for the first time. From the opening of the first of these fits it was quite clear that what I had in hand was not excised verses from the original poem, but an entirely new poem, a sequel to the first. The allusions to the wooden belfry above the hall staircase at Christ Church in the second fit probably date these fits shortly after the publication of the first *Snark* in 1876, for that belfry was obscured by the present stone tower in 1878. This is further suggested by a piece of evidence that I completely mis-interpreted in my talk to you two years ago. Henry Holiday's letter, in which he declines to illustrate the Bookman, was dated 30.2.1876, too late to be concerning the publication of the original *Hunting of the Snark*, which rolled off the presses just a month later. Clearly Holiday had been engaged to illustrate the sequel, and the Bookman fit is almost certainly part of that later, possibly unfinished poem. The mention of *The St. James's Gazette* in the second fit, however, suggests that Dodgson worked on these verses over a period of several years, for that paper was not founded until 1880 and Dodgson's first contribution came in 1881. My previously discovered fit "The Booking" may have been written before these opening fits, as it still includes The Boots as a character.

The two fits which are published here for the first time, the wittily named "The Recrewting," and "The Sailing," are filled with typical Carrollian allusions—from his barb at those would-be critics who attempted to read a meaning into his original nonsense to his humourous send-ups of Bishop Samuel Wilberforce and the Thirty-Nine Articles (though these two religious jokes may be part of why Dodgson never allowed these verses to see the light of day). He pokes fun at those who would challenge Euclidean mathematics and even revisits his own riddle of the stopped watch. Critical readers, no doubt, will find much more fodder for annotation and explication that I, a mere treasure hunter, am able to. With luck, on my next visit to Westhill, I may perhaps uncover the rest of Carroll's great unknown poem.

Charlie Lovett
21 January 2000

The Recrewting

"You must face up your Snark," the psychiatrist said,
  While the Bellman, reclined in a chair,
Felt a sinking sensation of panic and dread,
  Like a hamster with snakes in his hair.

"You must face up your Snark, I have said it twice,
  Yet you sit there perspiring and blue.
You must face up your Snark; I have said it thrice.
  I'm a doctor; you're sick; and it's true."

The Bellman knew well that a triptych meant truth,
  Though he wished for a simpler cure,
And he swallowed a teaspoon of salt and vermouth
  To give him the nerve for the tour.

He required a crew, this the Bellman knew,
  So he placed an advert in *The Times*:
"Several Snark Hunters Wanted—whatever you do
  Must begin with a 'B' and have rhymes."

The first applicant analysed novels and odes,
  And wrote critical essays for hire,
Filled with polysyllabic jargon and codes,
  Semi-colons, allusions, and ire.

He came as a Critic, and pompously cried
  To that sceptical leader of men,
He'd interpret the trip where the Baker had died,
  Before they went sailing again.

"You were searching for God and redemption by
grace,

You sought happiness, glory, and oil.

You were lost in the files of the Tichborne Case

You found emptiness, sorry, and toil."

"It's all nonsense, I tell you!" the Bellman exclaimed,

"We've no use for you here, leave us be.

And as far as the arrogant title you've claimed,

Doesn't 'Critic' begin with a 'C'?"

"But I'm brilliant, I'm brainy, and bona fide bright.

I've bonhomie and bravery, I'm buff!"

"You're bogus and boring, a blundering blight.

You're brooding and bug-eyed—a bluff."

The next was a Bard, who would quote from his plays

    In iambic pentameter verse,

Or recite dark soliloquies lasting for days,

    Or screech sonnets on deck, which was worse.

The Bellman removed him below to a cell,

    "More matter, less art," he decreed;

And the Bard worked not wisely, nor neither too well,

    At polishing forks they would need.

From the previous journey, the Broker explained

    He should like to join in on the next,

For the versified log of *that* Snark hunt contained

    No exploits of his in the text.

"I donated a saxophone played only thrice

By a Rugby first former; what's more,

Gave the Boots a bronze shovel, garnished with lice,

For his use as he rested on shore.

"From the Baker I purchased two pair of fine boots;

From the Barrister forty-two wigs;

From the Banker his set of six gold bandicoots;

From the Maker of Bonnets, twelve figs.

"Of my liberal largess to the crew, in the press

Only two blunt allusions are made:

I was brought through those woods to evaluate goods,

And at one point I sharpened a spade."

(To digress to the Boots, who had sharpened that
spade

With the Broker, his time's been well spent;

The chemists he's opened is said to have made

A return of ten thousand percent.)

"I feel like a pawn!" The Broker raved on,

And would surely be clamouring still,

But the Bellman submitted, and quickly admitted

He'd be lost without brokering skill.

A Bowler whose skill was remarkably small

Was the next to sign up for the ride;

He bowled forty-two overs, and every ball,

If long enough, would have been wide.

A great Benefactor donated the boat,

    And a thimble filled up with hard tack,

So the Bellman, who reckoned he'd keep them afloat,

    Packed him up below-decks in a sack.

A Bailiff who hoped he could handcuff their foe,

    Was engaged for his smiles and his charms.

While a Baggagemaster held a large portmanteau

    In each of his six burly arms.

A Bachelor allowed he would marry their prey,

    If he might take the Snark unawares,

And explained he'd prepared rather well for that day,

    By investing in Railway Shares.

The care that he showed in arranging their shelves

Earned a Bookman a place on the team,

For the crew knew full well if they did it themselves,

Things would seldom be quite what they seem.

A Badger, though gruff, was manly enough

To secure the last place on the hunt.

Though he couldn't make lace, one could tell by his

face

That his way with a Snark would be blunt.

Left behind on the dock were a sorrowful horde

Of those whom the Bellman declined:

A Boatswain (whose talents were useless on board)

And Bishop who'd been much maligned.

He at first had attracted the Bellman's remark,

Being soapy, and quite full of hope,

But the cruel appellation "Evolved from a Snark"

Had left him unable to cope.

A Baptist had happily boarded the ship,

'Til he learned that he must sign his name

To the thirty-nine rules which governed the trip,

And he said "I decline, just the same."

A Botanist claimed "My skills are self-taught,

I've discovered the ferns which Snarks eat."

But the six dozen monkeys, uncaged, that he brought

Gave the Bellman a case of cold feet.

A Beadle, a Beagle, a Beekeeper, too,

And a Bigamist with both his wives,

All waved from the shore at the vanishing crew,

Then turned, and went on with their lives.

The Sailing

The ship that they sailed was a second-hand yacht
 From the fleet of the Marquess of Bath.
Was Euclid consulted? Certainly not!
 For the vessel broke all laws of math.

At the top of the mast, two parallel lines
 Intersected each other quite nicely,
While forty-two digits and three porcupines
 Gave the value of pi quite precisely.

A vast outer jib which they called "Tweedledum"

Had a hypotenuse with rude airs—

Multiplied by itself it equalled the sum

Of Onslow and Bloomsbury Squares.

The Bellman removed from his waistcoat with flair

A watch filled with butter and wine,

And dusting the crumbs off with querulous care,

He announced that the time was "not nine."

The crew gathered round in amazement profound

At the time-piece, un-moved, on display;

While their watches and clocks suffered nautical

shocks,

The Bellman's was right twice a day.

"Nine o'clock's not the time to be plotting our course,"

Said the Bellman, his voice filled with glee,

So he pulled out his map, dusted off the remorse,

And asked the crew "what do you see?"

"It's a Lexicon," quietly grumbled the Bard.

"It's a hat-box or bathing-machine,"

Said the Bailiff, who'd foolishly lowered his guard

(so low it could hardly be seen.)

"I should call it a soap bar," the Badger declaimed,

But the Bellman just shook his head "No."

"Can't you see? It's a Belfry?" the Bowler exclaimed,

"Of the early debased style, you know.

"There was one near the meadow where I used to

    bowl,

    With identical angles and lines,

The result of the architect's rare self-control,

    Absent from all his other designs."

"'Tis the shape of a belfry, indeed," said the man

    Who had spread out the map for their view.

Such a spacious rectangle, I'm sure that we can

    Find the beast it's our job to pursue."

Their sails fluttered bright in the sharp morning light,

    In every shape Euclid allowed,

And quite a few more which if seen from the shore,

    He would certainly have disavowed.

"Gather round," cried the Bellman, "I've something to

say,"

And most of the crew paid him heed,

But the Bowler kept patiently bowling away,

(Though persistent, he did not succeed).

"You all know of the marks which identify Snarks,

And the way all such creatures are sought.

But whilst on vacation I found information

On just how a Snark must be caught.

"In the bowels of the Bodleian chained in the dark

Is a manuscript where I found writ,

The ancient instructions for hunting a Snark,

In a rare dialect of Sanskrit.

"We must seek it thimbles and seek it with care,

And pursue it with forks and hope.

We must threaten it's life with a Railway Share.

We must charm it with smiles and soap."

The great benefactor moaned with regret,

"Why that book was donated by me,

Those instructions appeared in the *St. James's*

Gazette,

In the 'Letters from Readers,' page three."

"But written below is a footnote, you know,"

Said the Bellman, quite bursting with pride

"And when its translated, you'll find explicated

The equipment required for Snarkcide.

"Most Snarks are all thumbs, thus the thimble
becomes
And essential device for the chase.
Though they dine in a group, Snarks never eat soup,
So a fork will suffice at its place.

"The creatures are horrible dancers, and known
To tread on one's feet when they lead,
And Boojums are specially accident-prone,
Which is why care is something we'll need.

"Postpartum depression is rife among Snarks
Of both genders; to help them to cope,
When we hear the soft sound of the juvenile's barks
We should ready our smiles and our hope.

"Though known to invest up to seventeen pence

In steamships and similar ventures,

Snarks have always avoided, with circumspect sense

The volatile railway indentures.

"They will buy up the patents for pills that grow hair,

As they skip and skedaddle with glee,

But wave in their face a foreclosed railway share,

And they cower with fear, don't you see."

The bold baggagemaster with six beefy arms

Interrupted the Bellman to state

He'd brought sixty-five stone of fresh soap, but no

charms.

"I was told that you'd use it for bait."

"Your portmanteaus filled up with soap, furthermore,"

The Bellman kept up his address,

"Are as useful as all that I've mentioned before,

And the key to our journey's success.

"For a Snark loves to bathe, as you're surely aware,

It will gyre in the water for hours,

And when Boojums are found in quartets or a pair,

They are waiting their turn in the showers.

"But the Snark's greatest sadness," the Bellman went
on

Though choked with the tears of emotion,

Is the lack of that mythical phenomenon

Known as bar-soap with lavender lotion."

"We shall bathe with the Snarks," cried the man with
the bags,
And he lifted a glass and imbibed.
"Let us chortle with joy, let us run up our flags,
For my soap is just as you've described."

They let out a cheer of outgrabing sincere,
And embraced their brave chief in profusion.
The Bellman then knew that he'd picked the right
crew,
In that moment of perfect confusion.

In the ensuing years only a few odd additional stanzas of Dodgson's alternative Snark have surfaced. We perhaps may never know the fate of that strange crew who set out with such high hopes and so many forks.

The Bard produced costumes, some props, and a
    script
    From voluminous velveteen sacks.
"'Tis time for the crewmen's rehearsal," he quipped,
    "Of *The Death of a Snark*" in five acts.

But the Bellman did claim, "It should be in my name,
    And not merely because of my rank.
For the Bard's lowly art was inspired by my chart,
    Look, all of his verses are blank!"

The boisterous bachelor, with slide rule in hand

Ascribed to the play a diameter,

While the bard misdirected his thespian band

In perfect iambic pentameter.

The Bachelor proposed that the Snark be ensnared

With rings of all sizes and shape

And perhaps with a sonnet, if one could be spared,

Without leaving the Bard in a scrape.

But the Master of Bags knew too well of such things,

From his decades in rail observation,

And no Kingfishing Snark, despite poems and rings

Would wed thus below of his station.

The bowler bowled furiously, bent on the bales,

But a boundary was 'snarked' with each ball.

First the boundaries of Ireland, Scotland, and Wales,

Then of good taste, of Magdalen, and Gaul.

They tied all nine flippers together with string.

They dipped both his wingtips in glue.

They filled up the pouch of his do-hickey-thing

With eleven half-pints of beef stew.

Forks and Soap

BY

BYRON W. SEWELL

Forks and Soap

*O*rans stepped out of the void, materializing in the gloomy foyer of Forks, a favourite watering-hole on the up-scale outskirts of Jabberwabber. His sudden translation was accompanied by a flash of bluish-white light, which no one in the restaurant paid any attention to whatsoever.

"Just one?" asked the greeter, a cute young thing covered in intricate emerald-green scales. She was wearing a Forks tee-shirt, which featured a cartoon of a Jubjub Bird playing an accordion and the words "POLKA TILL YOU DROP" emblazoned across the top. Krans liked her neon-yellow eyes, which seemed to glow in the semi-darkness of the foyer.

"Actually, there will be two of us," he replied and then growled softly to let her know that he found her attractive, even though he was at least sixty years her senior; once a flirt, always a flirt. "He will ask for Krans. Perhaps you can direct him to my table?"

She nodded. "Of course. Smoking or non?"

"Smoking, definitely!" Krans said, irritated that there was even a non-smoking section. He felt strongly that all public places should be smoker friendly.

"Follow me, please," she said as she turned to lead the way, swishing her tail with a provocative "snap" that sounded like a small firecracker going off. When he was seated she handed him a menu.

Forks was always crowded after 4:00 p.m., and didn't close until 3:00 a.m. There was a dirty sponge-rock band playing loud, discordant music—or perhaps more accurately, making a great deal of noise—on a small stage near the long, curving bar, which was already crowded. The music suited Krans; if there was anything he hated it was music with some insipid melody to it. The pink walls of the restaurant were festooned with thousands of forks—salad, dessert, spork, cheese, olive, oyster, pastry, pitch, tuning, barbecue, gig, trident—you name it—in all sizes, dates and materials—and all of them screwed securely to the walls to discourage theft. Ironically, customers had to eat with their hands, claws, sucker tubes, mouthparts, or hooves; cutlery (and chopsticks) were unavailable and customers were not allowed to bring their own.

Krans studied the menu, which was printed daily to reflect current market prices and availability. Forks specialized in sushi and ultra-fresh raw meat. Some of the mammalian and avian fare were delivered alive and then slaughtered in a special room behind the kitchen, so that the meat could be served still retaining some body heat. Stocks of fish and other sea creatures were kept alive in large tanks at the back of the restaurant. Snakes were kept in a deep pit in the floor of the kitchen. On rare occasion Forks would even offer higher primates, but the prices were outrageous and Krans seldom indulged in this extravagance; he was content with old-fashioned ibex, Indian rhino or bison. A waitress appeared in a thick cloud of invisible pheromones and smiled at him. "Hi, big fella! My name's Dayna; I'll be your server tonight. What can I get you to drink?"

Krans was stunned by her scent and fell instantly in lust with her; his nostrils instinctively flared to drink her in. Her fragrance made it difficult for him to concentrate, since his instincts tried desperately to override his rational mind, but he finally managed to say, "I'll have a bucket of iced Corona longnecks and a bottle of tequila."

"Any appetizer while you're waiting for your friend?"

"What have you got tonight?" he asked, drowning in her large, liquid eyes, which were set beautifully on the sides of her head, allowing her an almost 340-degree field of vision. He made a mental note that it would be almost impossible to sneak up on her, even in the dark; difficult, but perhaps not impossible.

"Tonight we're featuring fresh sea urchin. We've also got our standard Kreamy Krill soup, deviled raven eggs, extra-spicy ostrich wings, and..." She paused. "There's something else. Wait a minute! I'll think of it! Oh, yeah! Rocky Mountain oysters!"

"Everything sounds great! Can you do a sample platter for two?"

"Sure. It'll just take a few minutes to slap it together. I'll be right back with your drinks and a starter." She smiled provocatively, completely exposing her beautiful six-inch long canines.

Krans almost swooned, but finally managed to say, "Thanks, Dayna."

"No problem, Hon." She turned and hurried away, her ponderous weight rattling the dishes on the tables that she passed.

Her cloud of pheromones were steadily pulled up into the high-volume ventilation system along with the smoke, and after a few minutes Krans finally regained his ability to think clearly, the rush of his hormones subsiding. But it didn't last long. Dayna soon returned with his beer and tequila, once again engulfing him in a vapour cloud of nearly irresistible pheromones. She also brought along a two-quart yellow plastic bucket full of unusually large Rocky Mountain oysters.

"Here you go, Hon," she said brightly. "You can start with these babies. They're fresh from Montana."

"Thanks, Dayna," he finally managed to say, just as she left. He took a large pull on a beer, poured a half bottle of habanero sauce into the bucket, swirled them around, and then shoved his snout into the bucket, scarfing up a half-dozen oysters. He absolutely loved spicy-hot fat, and these were as close to perfection as he could imagine.

He was just starting on his second Corona when his friend walked up and slid into the booth on the opposite side of the table. "Hey, Boojum, ol' buddy!" he said, a bit too loudly. "How ya doin'?"

"I'm doing fine, Krans," he said as he reached across the table and they shook hands. "It's nice to see you."

"You too!" Krans shoved the bucket of half-eaten oysters across the table to him. "Here, try some of these," he said. "They're great! Nice and spicy!"

Boojum had his snout down in the bucket when Dayna reappeared. He pulled his head up when the pheromones hit him, instantly recognizing Dayna's unforgettable scent.

Boojum was a regular at Forks and the waitresses all knew him. Dayna grinned at him and asked, "What you drinkin' tonight, Boo?"

"I'll have what he's having," he said. "You sure smell good tonight, Dayna!"

She ignored this last remark; she had a splitting headache and just wasn't in the mood for breeding. "Coming right up," she said cheerfully. "And your appetizers will be right out." She turned and headed back to the kitchen.

"Let me see your menu, Krans," Boojum said. "Do they have anything interesting tonight?"

"Mostly the usual fare."

"I'm sorry I'm a bit late. I caught a human today and I just delivered him to the service entrance at the back. They paid me 500 Zurgs for him. Not bad!"

"Not bad at all!" Krans agreed. "Where'd you catch him?"

"I was over on Snark Island. I had seen a big ship and went up on a ridge to get a better view. I counted nine crewmen and a big rodent-looking animal that I couldn't see well enough to identify. The whole crew disembarked and came ashore. They seemed to be looking for something. I'm not sure what. There's no gold on the island, so I can't guess what it was.

Anyway, they all made their way slowly up the slope towards me. I could see that they were all armed with forks, but no guns. I decided that this might be a good opportunity to snag one or two of them, so I hid behind this big rock and waited. As they were making their way up I finally saw that the rodent was actually a beaver, so I figured these guys must be Canadians, which is good, since they're all pretty tasty, as you probably know."

"I've only ever tasted one Canadian," Krans said, "and he was pretty good; a little bony, but OK."

"Yeah, it depends upon where they come from. I'm not too fond of the ones from Quebec; they have a strong garlic taste that I don't care for. But I really like the ones from Ontario! They have a kind of pine-nut flavour to them."

"Yeah, I've heard that," Krans said.

"Anyway, I laid low and waited, and pretty soon this nice little fat one comes right around the rock. He smelled like a wedding cake, which was strange! Anyway, I grabbed him before he could say too much. It's a funny thing!"

"What is?"

"He seemed to know me, but I can't figure out how. I can't recall ever having met him, and I have a good memory for faces."

"Why do you think he knew you?" Krans asked.

"Just before I clamped my paw across his mouth, he cried out 'It's a Boo!'"

"No way!" Krans exclaimed. "Now that's really weird!"

"I know! It kind of rattled me. I decided I had better get out of there in case more of them recognized me, so I quick dove into the void."

Just then, Dayna showed back up and both Krans and Boojum swooned once again. This time she was carrying a huge platter stacked high with the appetizers Krans had ordered. "Here you go," she said. "By the way, we have an adjustment to the menu I need to tell you about."

"Don't tell me you're out of bison again!" Krans said. "That happened to me the last time I was here."

"No, no! We've got tons of bison back there! We've just got some fresh primate in!"

"How much does that cost?" Krans asked, sceptical that he could afford any of it.

"20 Zurgs for 10 zips."

"How much meat is that?" Krans asked.

"About enough for a decent sandwich," she said.

"That's not too bad! What kind of primate? I'm not too keen on monkey."

"You're in luck; this one's a human."

"Really?" Krans asked. She nodded. "OK, then I'll have five zips, just for a taste. I prefer thigh."

"You got it, Hon," she said. "How about you, Boo?"

"How much for the head?'"

"There's not much meat on it; mostly fat, bone and teeth. There's brains, of course, if your jaws are strong enough to

146

crack the skull open. And you get the tongue, of course. You can have the whole head for 5 Zurgs."

"OK." Boo said. "I'll have the head then."

"Right! I'll be right back," she said. "I need to go place your order before someone else gets it first. He won't last long at these prices!" She thundered away.

"I wonder if they're offering us that fat little Canadian that you just sold them; the one you caught on Snark Island?" Krans asked.

"Probably," Boo agreed.

"If he tastes like garlic I'm going to blame you!"

"He won't,'" Boojum assured him. "Like I said, he smelled like wedding cake."

"Maybe he just got married," Krans suggested.

"Naw! He's too ugly. More likely, he's a Baker."

"I hope so!"

"I've got something for you," Boojum said, reaching into a pouch he wore around his neck. He pulled out a small silver salad fork, which he handed to Krans.

"What's this?"

"It's the fork that my catch had in one hand when I caught him." He reached back into his pouch. "He had this in his other hand," he said as he shoved a small bar of soap across the table.

"What do you suppose he was doing with these?" Krans asked.

"I'm not sure, but it would appear that he might have been planning to eat the soap for lunch."

Fit for Purpose

"Just the place for a *Snark*!" the Bellman cried,
　As he ordered a book with care;
Completing the form the first time that he tried,
　At a price both good value and fair.

"Just the place for a *Snark*! I have said it twice;
　What I tell you this time is true!
Just the place for a *Snark*! Now I've told you thrice:
　There's but one *Snark* edition for you!"

"The Evertype book's the companion of choice,
　For completing this *Snarkasbord* view."
He repeated himself in a thunderous voice,
　"What I tell you again is true!"

The Bellman and ISBN 978-1-904808-36-7

ALSO AVAILABLE FROM EVERTYPE

Eachtraí Eilíse i dTír na nIontas, *Alice* in Irish, 2007

Lastall den Scáthán agus a bhFuair Eilís Ann Roimpi
Looking-Glass in Irish, 2009

Le Avventure di Alice nel Paese delle Meraviglie
Alice in Italian, 2010

L's Aventuthes d'Alice en Êmèrvil'lie, *Alice* in Jèrriais, 2012

Alicia in Terra Mirabili, *Alice* in Latin, 2011

La aventuras de Alisia en la pais de mervelias
Alice in Lingua Franca Nova, 2012

Alice ehr Eventüürn in't Wunnerland
Alice in Low German, 2010

Contoyrtyssyn Ealish ayns Cheer ny Yindyssyn
Alice in Manx, 2010

Dee Erläwnisse von Alice em Wundalaund
Alice in Mennonite Low German, 2012

L'Aventuros de Alis in Marvoland, *Alice* in Neo, 2012

Lès-Aventûres d'Alice ô Pèyis dès Mèrvèy,
Alice in Borain Picard, 2012

Ailice's Àventurs in Wunnerland, *Alice* in Scots, 2011

Alices Äventyr i Sagolandet, *Alice* in Swedish, 2010

Alice's Carrànts in Wunnerlan, *Alice* in Ulster Scots, 2011

Ventürs jiela Lälid in Stunalän, *Alice* in Volapük, 2012

Anturiaethau Alys yng Ngwlad Hud, *Alice* in Welsh, 2010

www.ingramcontent.com/pod-product-compliance
Lightning Source LLC
Chambersburg PA
CBHW030516260626
47157CB00005B/1763